DEMAGOGUERY

AND

DEMOCRACY

PATRICIA ROBERTS-MILLER

THE EXPERIMENT

NEW YORK

DEMAGOGUERY AND DEMOCRACY
Copyright © 2017 by Patricia Roberts-Miller
Paperback afterword copyright © 2020 by Patricia Roberts-Miller

First published in 2017 by The Experiment, LLC. This paperback edition first published in 2020.

The Experiment, LLC | 220 East 23rd Street, Suite 600
New York, NY 10010-4658 | theexperimentpublishing.com

THE EXPERIMENT and its colophon are registered trademarks of The Experiment, LLC. Many of the designations used by manufacturers and sellers to distinguish their products are claimed as trademarks. Where those designations appear in this book and The Experiment was aware of a trademark claim, the designations have been capitalized.

The Experiment's books are available at special discounts when purchased in bulk for premiums and sales promotions as well as for fundraising or educational use. For details, contact us at info@theexperimentpublishing.com.

Library of Congress Cataloging-in-Publication Data

Names: Roberts-Miller, Patricia, 1959- author.
Title: Demagoguery and democracy / Patricia Roberts-Miller.
Description: New York : The Experiment, 2017. | Includes bibliographical references.
Identifiers: LCCN 2017017587| ISBN 9781615194087 (hardcover) | ISBN 9781615194193 (ebook)
Subjects: LCSH: Rhetoric--Political aspects. | Political oratory. | Democracy.
Classification: LCC P301.5.P67 R64 2017 | DDC 320.973--dc23 LC record available at https://lccn.loc.gov/2017017587

ISBN 978-1-61519-676-0
Ebook ISBN 978-1-61519-419-3

Cover and text design by Sarah Smith

Manufactured in the United States of America

First paperback printing March 2020
10 9 8 7 6 5 4 3 2 1

To my students, past, present, and future

It's a commonplace that we live in an era of demagogues, and it's a commonplace that demagogues are successful because they mislead dupes and "sheeple" with what is obviously pandering, dishonesty, and irrational rhetoric. Demagogues sucker them. We're all agreed on that point. We just disagree with them, since those benighted fools think we're suckered by demagogues! Of course we aren't. That accusation just shows what mindless Flavor Aid drinkers they are. Our leaders are honest (even if sometimes mistaken), well intentioned, and authentic. Theirs are lying, malevolent, and manipulative. And we are in a terrible situation now because our political scene is dominated by their demagogues.

The underlying narrative is that our political culture has been damaged because a demagogue has arisen and is leading people astray. If we accept this narrative (one that doesn't actually hold up to scrutiny), then we try to solve the problem of demagoguery in ways that worsen it: We call for purifying our public sphere of *their* demagogues, often in very demagogic ways. That narrative misleads us because it reverses cause and effect. We don't have demagoguery in our culture because a demagogue came to power; when demagoguery becomes the normal way of participating in public discourse, then it's just a question of time until a demagogue arises. So, this book is not about a demagogue but demagoguery—how it works, how to describe and identify it, how good people can find themselves relying on demagoguery, and what we can do about it.

I've grown increasingly concerned about American political discourse since the days leading up to the 2003 invasion of Iraq. That was a time when demagoguery became the dominant approach to public discourse, and it echoed rhetoric from another tragedy from our past, when too many major political figures were engaged in defending slavery. It's easy, now, to say that it was wrong for so many smart people to support slavery. It gets a little more uncomfortable to admit that people defended slavery on the basis of belief systems many of us still have: that Christianity is moral, that the role of government is to maintain order, that people who are financially successful are somehow better than those who are unsuccessful, that government intervention is bad except when it isn't. But the fact is many smart people did defend slavery on those grounds.

Defenses of slavery weren't about some external reality of falsifiable facts but about an alternative "reality"—one created by powerful and respectable defenders of slavery. To take simply one example: In 1835, it was rumored that the American Anti-Slavery Society had flooded the South with copies of a particular pamphlet (they hadn't). When the

English writer Harriet Martineau traveled the region, she asked people if anyone had seen it, and didn't find anyone who had, although they all agreed the South had been flooded. William Gilmore Simms, a prominent author, condemned her argument as obviously wrong because she had believed abolitionists, whom he disliked and didn't respect, instead of "the first names in our country" (that is, the most powerful people in the South).* Simms didn't claim those "first names" had seen the pamphlets (nor did the prestigious people with whom Martineau spoke); he was saying that Martineau should have believed their version because they were people Simms respected. For Simms, the truth is determined by the identity of the people making claims, and it's possible to dismiss any claim simply on the basis of who is making the argument. Arguments for slavery weren't pragmatic or ethical

---

* William Gilmore Simms, *Slavery in America: Being a Brief Review of Miss Martineau on That Subject* (Richmond: T. W. White, 1838), 19.

discussions about the realities of slavery; they were assertions about abstract identities (The Slave, The Slave Owner, The Abolitionist) and performances of loyalty to the South. They were demagoguery.

The debate over whether to invade Iraq was disturbingly similar to the slavery debate—not so much what people were arguing, but the assumptions (and sometimes assertions) people were making about *how* to argue, and *how* to make political decisions. The argument was about loyalty and identity. Instead of engaging the arguments and evidence that were presented, too many people dismissed claims on the basis of who was making them, and dissent was treated as treason. It was demagoguery. There were two key arguments defending the invasion of Iraq. One was that Saddam Hussein presented an imminent threat to the United States (in many informational enclaves he was credited with having been behind the 9/11 terrorism) and that regime change (made possible by an invasion) was the only possible response to his threat, and the United States could achieve that regime change quickly and easily. The other argument was about argument itself. It characterized any argument about policy (whether, in fact, Iraq did have weapons of mass destruction and whether regime change could be effected through an invasion) as unnecessary, dithering, disloyal, and possibly even deliberately evil, since the correct course of action was so obvious. Major media outlets demonized dissent. In a democracy.

As it turns out, the dissenters and skeptics were correct about the WMD claims, the supposed connection between 9/11 and Iraq, and the feasibility of our plans. At his August 22, 2006, press conference, George W. Bush admitted that there were no weapons of mass destruction in Iraq, that Iraq did not have ties to Al-Qaida, and that it had not been involved in 9/11. Being proven wrong on that first argument, about Iraq, should have made us all more skeptical about that second argument, about argument. But the majority of media outlets, pundits, and politicians that had insisted on the *obvious* veracity of those (now admittedly false) claims haven't admitted they were wrong to have argued for silencing dissent and criticism nor retracted their accusations of treason and disloyalty. They haven't stopped presenting policy issues as zero-sum contests between the obviously good (us) and the obviously bad (them). They recanted the decision to invade, but they haven't recanted the demagoguery that got them there.

This isn't the conventional view of demagoguery. Conventionally, demagoguery is about passion, emotionalism, populism, and pandering to crowds. Thinking about demagoguery that way makes it likely that we won't notice when we are persuaded by and promoting demagoguery because it gives us criteria that enables us to see only *their* demagoguery. For the term "demagoguery" to be a useful one, it has to involve criteria that can be applied to us and them.

Demagoguery is about identity. It says that complicated policy issues can be reduced to a binary of us (good) versus them (bad). It says that good people recognize there is a bad situation, and bad people don't; therefore, to determine what policy agenda is the best, it says we should think entirely in terms of who is like us and who isn't. In American politics, it becomes Republican versus Democrat or "conservative" versus "liberal." That polarized and factionalized way of approaching public discourse virtually guarantees demagogues, on all sorts of issues, and in all sorts of directions. Demagoguery is a serious problem, as it undermines the ability of a community to come to reasonable policy decisions and tends to promote or justify violence, but it's rarely the consequence of an individual who magically transports a culture into a different world. Demagoguery isn't about what politicians do; it's about how we, as citizens, argue, reason, and vote. Therefore, reducing how much our culture relies on demagoguery is our problem, and up to us to solve.

That's a complicated–and uncomfortable–argument, and it's one that needs to start with an argument about what public discourse in a democracy should be, how we should (and shouldn't) define demagoguery, how demagoguery works, what a culture of demagoguery looks like, and what we can do about it.

I.
Democratic Deliberation

There is a tendency to talk as though identity politics is a new phenomenon, but there have always been people who want to reduce politics to identity. People all over the political spectrum will often insist that it's possible to accept or reject an argument purely on the basis of the person who makes it, which often means whether an advocate (or critic) is "liberal" or "conservative."

This reduction of complicated policy questions to whether liberals or conservatives are better has four troubling consequences.

1. One can look as though one is standing apart from the argument and taking an "objective" stance simply by saying "both parties are just as bad." That's reducing the complicated notion of "objective" to some vague sense of "not obviously partisan." It might be a very biased statement (e.g., the common comment that abolitionists and slaveholders were "just as bad"); it might not. Saying both parties are just as bad isn't objective; it's just a thing you say to make people think you're objective. It can be nothing more than an excuse not to get involved.

2. Partisans will try to appeal to the notion that political arguments are really about which group is better in order to dismiss criticism of their group. We might think that we can refute criticism by pointing out that "the other party does the same thing too." But whether the other party does it too is relevant only if we're arguing about which party is better, not which policies are better.

3. The underlying problem is that we aren't arguing policies; we're arguing about identities, and therefore compromise is never considered a principled realization that they might have some legitimate concerns. It is, at best, a Machiavellian strategy forced on us by the bad group.

4. Losing a political argument now has much higher stakes. It isn't just about whether you persuaded someone of the merits of your policy, but about whether you are a good person.

Democracy is a very old political model, 2,500 years old, in fact. So there is a lot of data about democracies—what they're good at, what they're bad at, when they succeed, why they fail. There are two different kinds of characteristics that scholars of democracies note: structural and rhetorical. Structurally, democracies succeed when there is a strong middle class, the police and the military are separate and under civilian control, due process is perceived as a "fairness" test that applies across groups, government has to respect some kind of "private" space into which it will not intrude *unless* the public good is at stake, and people get mad if political figures—whether their own chosen representatives or *those* people's representatives—appear to be untruthful or unfair. If people decide to see things as a zero-sum game—the more *they* succeed, the more *we* lose, and we should rage about any call made against *us*, and cheer any call made against *them*—then democracy loses.

Democracy depends on rhetoric—on people arguing with one another and trying to persuade one another. But as we all know, not all ways of arguing are the same, and, therefore, there have long been arguments about what kinds of rhetoric are good and what kinds are harmful. And as with the structural characteristics above, there are some broad principles about good rhetorical practices on which people have agreed. Essentially, public discourse about policies (what actions we should take) should favor inclusion, fairness, responsibility, self-skepticism, and the "stases" (or "stock issues").*

The inclusion rule, like every one of these principles, is simultaneously straightforward and complicated. The discussion should include all the people with relevant information, the people with variant perspectives, and, as much as is possible, the people who will be most affected. As much as possible, we try not to rely on secondhand (or third-hand) versions of what *they* think, and we try to be accurate about their points of view. Sometimes people have to be excluded from

---

* "Stases" is the plural of "stasis." In rhetoric, "stasis" means the stable point on which the disagreement hinges. It's like the hinge of a door—if there is no hinge, then the door just falls out of the wall, or it can't be moved at all. If you complain to an office mate that she throws things at your clients, and so your business is failing, and she responds with, "Well, *you* voted for a puppy-kicker," then the two of you have different stases. You are on the stasis of what helps or hurts the business, and she is on the stasis of which of you is a better human being. Many (perhaps even most) logical fallacies operate by shifting the stasis.

the conversation—particularly if they threaten violence (the fallacy called *argumentum ad baculum*), or if they are refusing to let people speak, or refusing to follow the rules of discourse. When exclusion happens (and it always has to happen to some extent, or we'd never finish the argument), it can't simply be on an us-versus-them basis. We have to exclude them on grounds we would think reasonable were we the ones being excluded.

That's an example of the fairness rule. Trying to be fair in an argument—enforcing rules, including the rule that the rules are applied to everyone equally—will lead to arguments about the rules. And that's a good sign. Participants often need to argue about how we should argue, what we will count as relevant evidence, what constitutes disruptive behavior or unfair moves, and what "stases" are the most relevant. In fact, *arguments about how we should argue* most interfere with demagoguery, especially if those arguments concern whether the rules are being applied to all participants equally—if argument by insult is allowed for *us*, then it is also permitted for *them*.* We also strive, to the best of our ability, to be fair to one another in terms of how we characterize or represent what others think. Sometimes that means making inferences—pointing out that our opposition is making an assumption we think is invalid—but we need to be responsible in how we make those inferences. We can be mean, angry, vehement, and highly critical, as long as we don't whine if they are just as mean, angry, vehement, and critical with us. And we need to take responsibility for what we say, in terms of things like "redeeming" our claims if they're challenged, trying to be accurate and honest, trying to ground our arguments in relevant

---

* I'm not suggesting that every discussion should have these qualities. It can be cathartic to sit around with friends and be wildly unfair about *them*. And sometimes it's useful to have a supportive group in which disagreement is discouraged. But those are cases of conversations that are *not* democratic deliberation. Just as American football and soccer have different rules, so do different kinds of conversations.

evidence and credible sources (more on that below), and acknowledging the logical premises and consequences of what we're arguing. We need to enter the conversation willing to be wrong, willing to admit the limits of our own knowledge, willing to reconsider our evidence, sources, and premises. That is self-skepticism.

As will be discussed later (because it's complicated), a lot of people assume an absolute binary between certainty and hippy-dippy relativism. They assume that you are either certain (in which case you are justified in acting on your beliefs) or you have no idea (in which case you aren't). In fact, we all operate in a world that has various degrees of uncertainty, some of which should make us pause, but most of which enable us to act because we are reasonably sure. The self-skepticism rule doesn't mean we should never act because we can't be certain, but it does mean we should, especially if the stakes are high, think about *how* we are thinking.

If we are disagreeing about a course of action, then we are in the realm of "policy deliberation," and there is a long-standing consensus about what stases are most helpful for trying to determine the best policies for a community. Productive policy deliberation involves arguing about the need (what the problem or ill is such that we need to change what we're doing) and various possible plans to address it. We must also argue about the causes of the problem, because, despite what a lot of people believe, the right solution is rarely obvious—solutions are directly related to the specific cause(s), and so we have to make sure we have the cause accurately described. If my tires are worn because they're old, then replacing them is a great plan; if they're worn because my alignment is off, simply replacing my tires is in the long run a very expensive solution. Before I replace the tires (plan), I should figure out why they're worn (cause). When we argue about need and its causes, we also identify an ill—that is, a problem that is significant and inherent to the situation (it won't go away on its own). If I go to a doctor with a lot of symptoms and propose that she give me antibiotics, the doctor needs to determine the cause of my symptoms; if the cause is a virus that will go away in a day, then my paying for antibiotics is unnecessary, and may even have unintended consequences, such as making me more resistant to antibiotics I might need later.

When we argue about possible plans, we need to consider the stases of solvency, feasibility, and unintended consequences. We need to talk about whether a plan solves the problem or ill that has been identified (new tires won't fix my alignment; antibiotics won't cure a cold), if the plan is practical, and if it might end up doing more harm than good. If Famous Politician presents a lot of statistics about how terrible crime is, and shows that most violent crimes are committed by males between the ages of sixteen and twenty-four, then he might propose the plan that we lock up all males when they turn sixteen and release them when they turn twenty-five. It might solve the problem, but it's not feasible, and the consequences would be worse than the problem.

Thus, one of the problems with demagoguery is that it breaks all these rules of public discourse. Demagoguery says that only *we* should be included in deliberation because *they* are the problem; we are essentially better, and they are essentially evil, so it would be wrong ("suicidal" is often the term) to treat them as we would want to be treated; the only rhetorical responsibility we have is to be loyal to the in-group; the only relevant stasis is need, which is reduced to questions of identity.

II.
How *Not* to Define Demagoguery

As long as there has been democracy, there has been demagoguery. It's a Greek term, and, initially, a "demagogue" simply meant a political leader who was not an oligarch—a populist. Some populists were good, and some were bad. Plutarch (around 100 CE) insisted on an absolute distinction between demagogues and statesmen, and Plutarch's distinction has stuck with us. He said demagogues are rhetors just looking out for themselves who pretend to be populists and who rouse the ignorant masses through appeal to emotion.

Plutarch was wrong. Very wrong.

Think about it this way. Were Plutarch right, then it would be easy to identify demagogues. But, oddly enough, it isn't. Or, more accurately, it's easy to look back at other times and say *they were* suckered by demagoguery; it isn't easy, however, for people to recognize when *we are* being suckered. We now look back at the killing of Jews for supposedly desecrating the host, or poisoning wells, or being part of a worldwide conspiracy with horror. We now know that slavery was indefensible, that segregation was bad, that we should not have allowed eugenicists to forcibly sterilize sixty thousand people for being "defective," that Japanese internment was a ghastly breach of everything that America is supposed to be, that lynching "uppity" non-whites is unquestionably evil, that sending Jews who had managed to escape Hitler's genocide back to Germany was an appallingly unethical thing to do. All of those things happened because people were persuaded by demagoguery; but, had they seen it as demagoguery, they wouldn't have been persuaded.

So, demagoguery works when (and because) we don't recognize it as such. Therefore, it can't be as easy to identify as Plutarch says.

Because demagoguery is so pervasive today, at this point you might expect me to make hyperbolic claims about the disastrous consequences of continuing in our current situation, then promise you the three simple tricks to solve it.

Nope. While demagoguery is often disastrous (e.g., the Holocaust), it isn't always (e.g., hyperbolic rhetoric in YouTube comments, say, about the culturally disastrous consequences of some musical artists). And what it is, how to define it, how it operates, why people like it, what to do about it—all of those things are complicated. Demagoguery wouldn't exist if they weren't. The conventional definition of demagoguery as obviously false rhetoric on the part of corrupt and self-serving political elites who are manipulating their followers suggests that all we have to do is ask ourselves four questions about a rhetor:

1. Is what the person is saying obviously false?

2. Is the person bad?

3. Is the person appealing to populist notions?

4. Is the person being manipulative?

These are entirely the wrong questions to ask because we are, as I'll show, effectively asking ourselves if we like someone whom we think is like us and dislike people who are opposed to us. These questions won't help us see when *we* are being misled.

Demagoguery is comfortable because it says that the world is very simple, and made up of good people (us) and bad people (them).* The truth is obvious to good people

---

* There are several situations in which demagoguery admits complexity. For instance, if a central claim has been proven undeniably false, or a policy has been an obvious disaster, *then* demagogues will excuse their bad decision on the grounds that the situation was, unbeknownst to them, complicated. There is never an

like us, and you don't need to listen to anyone
who disagrees. In fact, we are in a bad situation
because we have listened to *them* too much in
the past, been too kind to them, and too compassionate. Demagoguery says we don't have
to debate *policies*, since what we should do is
empower good people (or a good person) to
do what every good person recognizes to be
the obviously right course of action; we need

---

admission that others said at the time it was complicated, nor a sense that we should move forward more willing to admit complexity in common decisions. When
various political figures, pundits, and media who had
supported the Bush plan as the *obviously* right thing
to do (and condemned all questioning or dissent as
treason) had to admit that the Iraq invasion had not
been a good idea, many claimed that they had been
opposed all along (even in the face of video and writ-
ten evidence that they had supported the invasion), or
they blamed Bush, or they admitted a lack of knowledge. They didn't go on to change how they advocated
for other policies, reconsider the very notion of "obviously" superior plans, or even reduce their screams
of treason at anyone who disagrees with them. The
second kind of case in which demagogues will admit
complexity involves conspiracy theories, which can be
very elaborate but ultimately make the case that the
cause of problems is simply the conspiracy.

to stop thinking and debating and just act.

In reality, political problems are complicated in their cause and cure, and there is no such thing as a perfect decision. While some plans are better than others, every one has costs and consequences, not all of which we can predict ahead of time. We're always going to be at least a little bit surprised by how things turn out, sometimes very surprised, even if we felt certain at the moment we made the decision. We are all wrong at some times and to some degree. A person who claims never to have been wrong is simply a person with a very convenient memory.

If we want to think of ourselves as people with good judgment, or if ambiguity and complexity make us uncomfortable, it will be painful for us to look back at decisions and acknowledge our own participation in the mistake. We will face substantial cognitive dissonance between our view of ourselves as good people with good judgment and an assessment of our past actions that acknowledges the mistakes. Demagoguery helps resolve that cognitive dissonance by telling us that we can stop questioning ourselves and our judgment—we didn't do anything wrong; we were absolutely right in our decisions. We are the real victims here.

When we look back at famous moments of demagoguery in the past, we think we would never have gotten suckered because we can look at what the demagogues were saying and see that it was obviously false. The Holocaust was not necessary self-defense, Germany was not a victim entitled to world domination, Japanese internment was not our only protection against invasion, eugenics was not going to reduce crime, segregation was not justified by science or Scripture, slavery was neither a necessary evil nor a positive good. But what we don't often do is imagine ourselves back in the moment and try to understand whether, in that time and with the information people had, we would have come to the same judgment as we do now. We don't want to admit that smart and good people liked Hitler, or thought he was raw and crude but would be matured by responsibility, or that he didn't really mean what he said, or that liberal democracy was dead and therefore fascism was the best choice, or that he could be controlled. Many smart people who didn't want genocide stoked the fires of hatred, thinking it was a controlled burn. It wasn't.

If this all sounds like an endorsement of some kind of historical determinism, or hippy-dippy relativism, it's not. Many smart and good people also opposed all of those policies, saw the problems with Hitler, and recognized the trouble that was brewing. My point is that being smart and good isn't enough to guarantee that we aren't falling for demagoguery. The world is not divided into good people (like us) who never engage in demagoguery and bad people (them) who do. We can't determine whether rhetoric is demagoguery by deciding whether the rhetor is a "good" or "bad" person. To judge their rhetoric, we have to look at their rhetoric.

Take, for instance, the support of Earl
Warren, then attorney general of California,
for the mass incarceration of people of Japanese ancestry in the spring of 1942. Warren
was a good person, heroic for his later work
on the Supreme Court in regard to segregation (*Brown v. Board of Education*), but his
testimony before the congressional committee concerning the proposed "evacuation"
of enemy nationals was later characterized
by the Commission on Wartime Relocation
and Internment of Civilians as "nothing but
demagoguery."* And, as will be shown later,
it was. But the four questions mentioned
above wouldn't have helped Warren, or anyone else at the time, to see his testimony as
demagoguery.

---

* United States Commission on Wartime Relocation
and Internment of Civilians, *Personal Justice Denied:
Report of the Commission on Wartime Relocation and
Internment of Civilians* (Washington, DC: Civil Lib-
erties Public Education Fund; Seattle: University of
Washington Press, 1997), 97.

1. Is what the person is saying obviously false? He wasn't presenting information he knew to be false; he thought it was true.

2. Is the person bad? The example of Warren shows why this question is useless for noticing that *we* are falling for demagoguery, since we would never answer that question about ourselves in the affirmative. Warren certainly didn't see himself as a bad person, and he sincerely meant well for his community.

3. Is the person appealing to populist notions? Warren's argument, as will be shown, relied on supporting testimony from law enforcement officers and on maps showing ownership patterns. While the notion that "the Japanese" were inherently untrustworthy was a popular belief, he wasn't acting as a populist, but as an elite expert.

4. Is the person being manipulative? Again, he was sincere and honest. And wrong.

A useful set of questions to ask wouldn't just enable people years later to see what mistakes were made; hence, this isn't a useful set. So what would be?

III.
What Demagoguery Is

If we're going to admit that demagoguery isn't obvious, that it isn't a black-or-white issue but rather exists on a range, then we're going to have to develop a more rigorous test for demagoguery than the above four questions. As befits someone skeptical of demagoguery, I'm not going to say that my definition is the only possible way to think about the problem. I'll propose an abstract definition, a set of criteria by which we can measure how demagogic a text, media outlet, or culture is, and an explanation of how demagoguery works. Here's the general definition:

Demagoguery is discourse that promises stability, certainty, and escape from the responsibilities of rhetoric by framing public policy in terms of the degree to which and the means by which (not whether) the out-group should be scapegoated for the current problems of the in-group. Public disagreement largely concerns three stases: group identity (who is in the in-group, what signifies out-group membership, and how loyal rhetors are to the in-group); need (the terrible things the out-group is doing to us, and/or their very presence); and what level of punishment to enact against the out-group (ranging from the restriction of the out-group's rights to the extermination of the out-group).

There are certain characteristics that are always present in the most extreme instances of demagoguery. These can serve as criteria for seeing where something is on a continuum of demagoguery. Demagoguery

- polarizes a complicated political situation into us (good) and them (some of whom are deliberately evil and the rest of whom are dupes);

- insists that, since the world can be reduced to those who are with us and those who are against us, to determine policy, we shouldn't argue policies as policies (that is, in terms of need, feasibility, solvency, and other "stases" discussed below) but should instead argue about identity (whether this policy is advocated by us or them) and motive (which necessarily means that demagoguery is generally "motivism," discussed below);

- presents the situation of the in-group (us) as so dire that we are justified in any actions, deeming values such as fairness across groups (that is, holding the in-group and out-group to the same standards) unnecessary and possibly suicidal;

- insists that the Truth is easy to perceive and convey, so that complexity, nuance, uncertainty, and deliberation are cowardice, dithering, or deliberate moves to prevent action ("naïve realism," explained below);

- relies heavily on fallacy, particularly straw man, projection, appeal to inconsistent premises, and argument from personal conviction;

- is not necessarily emotional or vehement, but places considerable emphasis on the "need" portion of policy argumentation (economic problems, terrorism, crime), often with implicit or explicit threats that "we" (the in-group) are faced with extermination, emasculation, and/or rape.

IV.
How Demagoguery Works

Above are the defining characteristics of demagoguery. They're always present to some degree in a demagogic text, argument, or culture, or it isn't demagoguery. The most important of all these characteristics is the reduction of political questions to us versus them. Social psychologists call this "in-group favoritism." They use the terms "in-groups" (us) and "out-groups" (them), which they refer to as "social groups." In-group favoritism is key because many, if not most, of the remaining characteristics of demagoguery in this book are essentially versions of, or direct results of, this simplification to us versus them. These characteristics don't have to be present for demagoguery to exist, but they often are.

One such characteristic is that *social group membership suffices as proof.* To give just one example, people will often reject a source as "biased" on the grounds that the author is a member of an out-group, as though group membership is sufficient proof of bias (that's called the "genetic fallacy").

We don't realize we're engaged in the genetic fallacy because it appeals to our (often incorrect) intuition that people like us (members of the in-group) are essentially trustworthy, and people like them (members of out-groups) are not. When we operate that way, we aren't just treating members of in-groups and out-groups differently; we are perceiving them differently. For instance, we have a tendency to attribute good motives to members of the in-group, and bad motives to members of the out-group, *for exactly the same behavior.* So, if an in-group political figure kicks a puppy, she was mistaken, or meant well, or the puppy deserved it, or we might even try to find ways to say it wasn't *really* kicking. If an out-group political figure kicks a puppy, it's proof that he is evil and hateful and that's what they're all like. If an out-group political figure saves a drowning puppy, she just did it to get votes. If an in-group political figure does it, the incident is proof that people like us are just plain better. *Our* politician who says something untrue is mistaken; *their* politician is deliberately lying. When their president issues a lot of executive orders, it's a sign of impending fascism; when our president does it, it's a sign of decisive leadership.

Group membership, then, can *seem* to serve as a kind of "proof"—without our noticing that our proof is actually our conclusion, that we have a circular argument impervious to disproof. One can see this circularity especially in regard to the popular notion of "bias"—whether a piece of information is "biased" or "objective" is often determined by our asking ourselves whether it's true.

If you spend as much time as I do crawling around the Internet arguing with extremists, you quickly learn the "that source is biased" move. You present a piece of evidence, and the person won't even look at it because, they say, *that* source is biased. The person making the "biased" accusation doesn't show the source is biased by offering a close analysis of how evidence has been misrepresented–the "bias" is deduced from the in-group/out-group membership. That source must be out-group, since it disagrees with in-group claims. It's a tight circle–a person can dismiss all disconfirming evidence on the grounds that it's disconfirming.

Many people believe that it is both possible and desirable to perceive the world exactly as it is, with no mediation; the most "objective" view is the one with the least interpretation, a mental state to which one can will oneself largely by rejecting complicated thinking about the situation. This model of perception (called "naïve realism" by social psychologists) assumes that, to determine if a claim is true, I simply need to look around my world and see if my perceptions confirm that it is true.

Naïve realism gives preference to simple explanations (since they are most likely to correspond to direct perception) and increases the tendency toward confirmation bias (since people tend to perceive more easily and quickly any information that confirms their current beliefs). Thus, paradoxically, the belief that one is the sort of person who always sees the world exactly as it is increases the likelihood not just of being wrong, but of being wrong in the same ways and about the same things again and again.

In addition, because naïve realists deny that they are looking at the world from a particular perspective (let alone mediated), they see no need to learn how to look at things from the perspective of other people (in fact, they often believe they can see all perspectives from their position). Their experience is normal and universal; other perspectives are special and particular and prejudiced. Thus, if they like kicking puppies, then everyone does; if they meet someone who doesn't like kicking puppies, that person is the exception who doesn't need to be considered. That sort of person, literally, doesn't "count" when naïve realists make assertions about people—they don't count the "exception" when they say "everyone"—and so a naïve realist can easily dismiss any disagreement.

Naïve realists often also rely on binaries—they divide things into this or that, with nothing in between. This reasoning through binaries reinforces naïve realism. They often believe that either you think the Truth is obvious (naïve realism) or you're saying that there is no Truth (sometimes called "relativism," or, even more inaccurately, "postmodernism"). There is either certainty or cluelessness. But that isn't generally the case; we spend a lot of time making decisions in situations of varying degrees of uncertainty. If there is a 90 percent chance of rain, we can feel fairly sure we should take an umbrella, and if there is a 1 percent chance of rain, we can feel comfortable leaving it behind, but we can't be similarly confident about either decision if there is a 50 percent chance of rain. Yet even if the rain chance is 50 percent, we are generally able to make a decision and take the umbrella or not; we don't stand in the doorway unable to move (in fact, if we did, we would report this behavior to a doctor, recognizing it as concerning). Our ability to think and act in probabilistic situations shows that the binary between naïve realism and relativism is false.

Another important binary that encourages people to avoid policy deliberation is between "good" and "bad" decisions. When we have been persuaded by demagoguery to take a particular course of action, we often quickly get feedback that it was a bad decision. The Nazis, for instance, got considerable blowback after Kristallnacht (the night of November 9, 1938, when Jewish businesses and synagogues were attacked), and the United States almost immediately faced insurgency when it invaded Afghanistan in late 2001. If we think all decisions are either entirely good or entirely bad, then how do we understand a decision we've made? If we didn't take an umbrella, and it begins to rain, then assuming that there is a binary between good decisions (the kind that good people make) and bad decisions (the kind that bad people make) leaves us with limited options. We can decide it was a bad decision, and try to get an umbrella, but that would be an admission that we made a bad decision, and that makes us bad people. We can reconsider our binary of good/bad decisions and the assumed connection to good/bad people. Or, we can insist that it was good (and stick with it and still refuse to get an umbrella). The third option is surprisingly attractive and common because the tendency we have to assume a binary between good and bad decisions makes it *harder* for us to learn from previous decisions or correct our course.

Thinking in these binaries makes us pant for the certainty and evasion of responsibility provided by demagoguery. To criticize naïve realism is not to say we can never be right or do right, or that there is no such thing as right and wrong. What criticizing naïve realism does suggest, and the reason that criticism is terrifying for some people, is that feeling certain is not the same thing as being right.

While demagoguery can be invoked anywhere along the political spectrum, and on nonpolitical issues, it most easily aligns with some version of what the linguist George Lakoff has called "strict father" model and some scholars call authoritarianism. The notion is that a good government acts like a strict father, training its children (citizens) through control and punishment to follow the rules established by the father. Lakoff has pointed out that there are metaphors that operate as binaries of control/ chaos, domination/submission, punishment/ reward. Particularly important to strict father model and authoritarianism is that believing and thinking are conflated—there is little or no praise for self-reflective critical thinking, and questioning authority is seen as rebellion. In this world, obedience to authority is always good. And there is a perfect binary between submission and resistance. Not to submit is to rebel. Declining to participate, asking that we listen to all points of view, wanting time to think through options, trying to discuss flaws in in-group plans and policies—these are all kinds of insubordination, rebellion, and disloyalty.

Authoritarianism can look antiauthoritarian by insisting on resistance to *their* authorities (who are illegitimate), but it always demands complete submission to *our* (legitimate) authorities. This argument about legitimate versus illegitimate authority is crucial to demagoguery's representation of its violence as necessary and noble self-defense. And the argument that *their* authority is illegitimate is made in two ways, both circular. First, their authority is illegitimate because they aren't really from here, they aren't really loyal to our values, they don't clearly demonstrate submission to the symbols and signs of what we consider *true*

Americans, Christians, Pastafarians, and so on. But all those arguments about loyalty are simply a complicated way of saying *they are not us*; their authority is illegitimate because they are they.

Second, *they* are using their authority to do things to which we object in principle. Never mind that we look the other way when our side does the same thing. When the GOP finds a filibuster useful, Democrats claim that the process is outrageously illegitimate; when the Democrats use it, the GOP insists they object to the filibuster in principle. So, really, neither party objects to the *principle* of the filibuster; the other party's use of authority is illegitimate because *they* are they.

Demagoguery does sometimes appeal to "traditional" authorities, or draw authority from what are presented as traditional ways of doing things. But those supposedly traditional values and practices are often of very recent origin, as in arguments about companionate marriage, the concept of race, the free market. "Traditional" can be another way of saying "how I was raised."

Equating "what I think of as traditional" with "what has a long history" is one of the ways that demagoguery often relies on a "universalized nostalgia." Rhetors using demagoguery will often talk about how things have "always" been done, and our need to return to how things "used to be," when "always" and "used to be" are mythologized versions of the in-group's youth. As in the case of arguments about marriage, what is a very recent invention, companionate marriage (a marriage between two individuals, grounded in romantic love), is projected through all time, and an era with a fairly high rate of problematic marriages (the 1950s) is filtered with a golden glow. When challenged about the accuracy of their history, a challenge that is often made on the basis of empirical evidence, and to which empirical evidence should be the response, people drawn to demagoguery will often respond in one of three ways: argument from personal conviction, identity as logic, or deductive reasoning.

If I say, "Squirrels are trying to get to the red ball," you might say, "How do you know that?" I might answer with citations of studies, quotes from squirrels, and quotes from squirrel experts. Or I might say, "Because I'm certain," which is an *argument from personal conviction*; I am presenting my certainty as evidence for you to believe something. Asking that you believe me isn't necessarily a fallacy. If I am a squirrel, an expert on squirrels, or have attended a lot of squirrel meetings, then I am asking you to accept my epistemic authority; my specific expertise is being presented as the basis of my claim. But what if I'm not an expert and haven't done any of those things? My personal conviction—not my expertise—is presented as though it's adequate. I am presenting myself as a *knower*, purely on my identity.

And so we're back to *us*, and the notion that in-group membership is the same thing as being right. Or, *identity as logic.* Probably the most complicated aspect of demagoguery to describe is how identity functions. The central presumption behind demagoguery—and the most attractive promise it makes—is that our current ways of categorizing people (such as gender, race, nationality, religion) are woven into the fabric of the universe. Those categories are, and should be, a hierarchy; some people are entitled to more goods than others by virtue of being better—they are better by virtue of having a certain identity, regardless of their behavior. Hence, paradoxically, members of the in-group (by virtue of being inherently "better" people) are held to lower standards, and can behave worse than members of out-groups.

Arguments from identity, or from conviction, aren't always demagogic—sometimes it's necessary to say, "Just believe me on this one." But they're problematic because they're hard to dispute. If someone says, "I am certain this is true, and that I am certain is the only evidence I am going to give you," then we're not in the realm of argumentation. It might still lead to a good conversation, one that's interesting and worth continuing, but we're having a different kind of conversation from democratic deliberation—it might be expressive, for instance. If that's *always* how someone participates in disagreements, then it's a problem, and then it's demagoguery.

Although it's conventional to say that demagogues lie, demagoguery has a complicated relationship with honesty. Demagoguery typically invokes language of certainty, accuracy, truth, authenticity, objectivity, and "facts." And I think people engaged in demagoguery are generally perfectly sincere, and may not feel that they're lying. Demagoguery is most effective when people conflate authenticity, sincerity, trustworthiness, and being truthful—but they aren't the same. A person can be perfectly sincere while telling a lie, and sincerely state something that is inaccurate. A sincere person who keeps getting information wrong isn't trustworthy.

When demagoguery does involve policy argument, the claims are generally deduced from important in-group values, rather than grounded in falsifiable studies or multipartisan scholarship. For instance, in the United States, pro-slavery rhetors argued that emancipation *must* result in a race war, although that hadn't happened in the states that had had emancipation. I once found myself in an odd argument with a fellow Christian who kept insisting that Christianity had a better record on slavery than any other religion because a religion that believed all men are made in God's image *must* treat all people more equally. He was unfazed by my pointing out the considerable body of evidence (including a website that had a lot of antebellum sermons promoting slavery) that showed a strong connection between Christianity and slavery. He rejected the actual historical

record in favor of a "fact" he deduced *must* be
true from his premise that Christian cultures
are necessarily better behaved than others.*

That may seem like simply a bad argument, but it didn't seem like a bad one to him
because it fit his notion about how to argue—
deduce from premises central to in-group
identity. I've had the same kind of argument
with people who contend that shifting decisions to the free market *must* work because
the market is rational, cheerfully ignoring
the examples of irrational market actions.
Arguments about "natural" health remedies
often adhere to the same logic—non-falsifiable
chains of reasoning that follow from the premise that "natural" is always and necessarily better. The argument that someone cannot have
done something racist because he or she is
not racist is a similarly deductive argument.

---

* That the premise—men are made in God's image—is
shared with the two religions he insisted *must* have a
worse record just made the whole argument even more
confusing.

Deductive arguments aren't necessarily bad (I'm not deducing a claim about all arguments from my premise that deductive arguments are bad), but they're problematic when they are set up in a way that *all* disconfirming examples can be rejected. This type of deductive reasoning is not a way of participating in argumentation—it's just a way of showing in-group loyalty.

Many scholars of demagoguery note its reliance on scapegoating and projection. Demagoguery scapegoats a particular *them* for the problems of the community as a whole; it might be something for which that group isn't at all responsible, or is only partially responsible (perhaps less than the in-group). For instance, Hitler scapegoated "the Jews" for Germany's having lost World War I, something for which they bore no responsibility, and England and France for starting World War II. Certainly, the war wouldn't have happened had England and France decided to allow Germany to keep conquering other countries, but the main responsibility was Hitler's. Scapegoating is closely related to projection, in which a rhetor condemns someone for what he or she is doing. This step is absolutely necessary for scapegoating (that is, for holding some group responsible for the in-group's problems). Projection has several forms, two of which are important here: the fallacy of false equivalence, and cunning projection.

Because demagoguery relies on and reinforces binaries, then actions are either good or bad, rather than lying somewhere on a range. Thus, since kicking puppies is bad, and failing to pet puppies is also bad, we might insist (and even sincerely believe) that criticism of *our* candidate for kicking puppies every day can be dismissed on the grounds that *their* candidate once failed to pet a puppy. (This is also sometimes called the fallacy of *tu quoque*–Latin for "you too!" Thus two very different things are treated as though they are the same–*the fallacy of false equivalence.*)

Condemning the out-group for the same thing the in-group does effectively distracts onlookers, making it complicated for them to figure out the cause and effect. For instance, demagoguery that condemns out-group self-defense as "just as bad" as in-group offensive violence necessitates that onlookers investigate the chain of events carefully enough to figure out who was the attacker, how much violence there was, what kind it was, who engaged in it, and other details that in-group media will almost certainly not provide. Since onlookers generally don't want to go to that trouble, they are likely to make the determination on the basis of which party seems more likable. Projection is a normal human tendency, but *cunning projection* happens when the projection is strategically beneficial, either by distracting the audience from the rhetor's flaws, or by keeping the attention on how bad *they* are.

When cunning projection is most effective, rhetors manage the condemnation of a group who has done little or nothing compared to what they have done (what the psychologist Gordon Allport called the "mote-beam" projection, in which you condemn someone for doing something when you're doing it even more). Even if it doesn't achieve that end, cunning projection generally muddies the waters enough that the in-group can continue its policies, as onlookers are prone to declare a pox on both houses.

If condemnation of out-group behavior is performed by a very likable persona, then onlookers are likely to conclude that the rhetor would never engage in the behavior she or he is condemning. This maneuver is especially effective with people who believe that you can know what someone believes by listening to what values he or she claims to espouse, and with people who think you can predict behavior by listening to values talk (who believe that "good" people—that is, people who say the right things—don't do "bad" things). This focus on the identity of the rhetor is tightened in situations of *charismatic leadership*.

The sociological conception of charismatic leadership has been muddied by the use of the term in business to mean something very different (simply a leader who is inspirational and thereby gets a greater level of commitment to a vision). The German sociologist Max Weber described three sources of power for leaders: traditional, legal, and charismatic. Traditional leaders can gain compliance from the people on the grounds that there is a tradition of following them—their power is limited by what that tradition is and how passionately people follow it. Legal authority, obviously, comes from what the laws say leaders can and can't do, and gives them specific powers of coercion. Charismatic authority is, Weber says, the least stable. It's at play in situations in which people give power to a leader because they believe he or she has almost supernatural powers (or supernatural powers have chosen this leader).

As the scholar Ann Ruth Willner says, charismatic authority "derives from the capacity of a particular person to arouse and maintain belief in himself or herself as the source of legitimacy."* Willner says that the charismatic leadership relationship has four characteristics:

1. The leader is perceived by the followers as somehow superhuman.

2. The followers blindly believe the leader's statements.

3. The followers unconditionally comply with the leader's directives for action.

4. The followers give the leader unqualified emotional commitment.†

---

* Ann Ruth Willner, *The Spellbinders: Charismatic Political Leadership* (New Haven and London: Yale University Press, 1984), 4.

† Ibid., 8

Charismatic leadership satisfies our desire to be part of something bigger, and, paradoxically, to hand all power over to someone else can make us feel more powerful because we think that person is a best version of ourselves. We feel that we have gained "agency by proxy." We have also dumped all responsibility for decisions onto the leader—what Erich Fromm, the scholar of Nazism, called an "escape from freedom." When we are in a charismatic leadership relationship, our sense of self-worth gets attached to the identity of the leader, so that we take personally any criticism of that leader, and have as much difficulty admitting flaws or errors on the leader's part as we do on our own. Because we see the leader as us, and we see us as good, we simply can't believe that he or she might do bad things. Hitler's architect and interior designer, Gerdy Troost, explained why she refused to believe that Hitler knew about the Holocaust: "How can a person who can be so kind, so attached to his dog, who can look at a child with such love, who can stand before a work of art and contemplate it with such feeling, how can such a person be a murderer? [....] It is inconceivable to me."*

It may be counterintuitive, but the charismatic leadership relationship is *strengthened* by the leader behaving erratically, making what might appear to be irrational arguments, judging situations quickly without much information (especially without expert advice), and making hyperbolic claims (especially about his or her own achievements and, oddly enough, health). Followers don't expect charismatic leaders to be responsible for what they say, nor to behave responsibly (in the ways described before—trying to be accurate, acknowledging logical implications and consequences); their *irresponsible* behavior is part of their power. Their use of hyperbole and tendency to be unfiltered in speech are taken to signify their passionate commitment to the in-group.

---

* Quoted in Despina Stratigakos, *Hitler at Home* (New Haven: Yale University Press, 2015), 140.

Demagoguery favors charismatic leadership, and, when demagoguery is culturally common, it is merely a question of time before all political figures within the same culture are performing various kinds of charismatic leadership roles—becoming the kind of people conventionally seen as demagogues. Hence, given enough time, demagoguery inevitably leads to the rise of demagogues.

Another striking characteristic of demagoguery is how much it is a rhetoric of victimization. *We* are being victimized by the situation (often by being treated the same as the out-group, so there is a kind of political narcissism operating), and *we* have so far responded to this victimization with extraordinary patience and kindness. If the actual history is disenfranchisement and violence, then that behavior is reframed as patience and kindness because it could have been worse.

Thus, for instance, advocates of segregation claimed that they were being victimized by the "Marxist" Supreme Court because they were being forced to obey laws they didn't want to obey. Of course, that's exactly what segregation was all about—forcing others, by disenfranchising them, to obey laws not of their own making. Homophobic demagoguery often alludes to the possibility of the in-group being victimized by unwanted sexual overtures, not because those rhetors are opposed to unwanted sexual overtures on principle (it's not uncommon for these same rhetors to object to prohibitions against sexual harassment), but because they are opposed to being the *object* of them.

As a consequence, demagoguery has to find a way to manage fear while not looking fearful (since fearfulness is somewhat confusingly assumed to be paired with thinking and deliberating). That such a task is pretty nearly impossible means there is a lot of cognitive dissonance in consumers of demagoguery about whether the in-group is brave or fearful. That dissonance is sometimes managed by claims of extraordinary courage in the face of a terrible situation, or a representation of oneself as calm and reasonable while making apocalyptic predictions, and the odd insistence that clearly hyperbolic claims are rational—as when claims arose that Obama was going to knock down everyone's door the day after his inauguration in order to confiscate guns. (I will admit, this is one aspect of demagoguery that often makes me laugh.)

The fearmongering can work only if the in-group perceives it's in danger of extermination, but demagoguery typically also includes claims that our triumph is predestined. This claim of predestination conflicts with claims mentioned above that we are threatened with extinction. If our triumph is predestined, then we aren't really in danger. There is a kind of *flickering determinism* to demagoguery. Victory is assured *and* we might be annihilated. That the in-group is in danger of extermination is used to rationalize exterminationist policies against the out-group; that we are in a state of war (which *they* started) means that we should not "do unto others as you would have them do unto you." Demagoguery either denigrates fairness as suicidal or reframes "fairness" as the in-group getting more. That is, instead of a "fair" situation being one in which everyone (in-group and out-group) is held to the same legal, ethical, and rhetorical standards, it is one in which the in-group is held to different standards because of our being essentially good. We don't generally see that we're holding ourselves to lower standards because of the strategy (mentioned earlier) of explaining the behaviors differently—we are frugal, but they are misers; we misspoke, but they lied.

Finally, demagoguery's displacement of policy argumentation with issues of identity explains the odd role that "authenticity" plays in communities subsisting on demagoguery. In such a world, a leader who says that things are complicated, that there isn't an easy solution, that we have made mistakes, and who argues for a slow, nuanced, and inclusive consideration of all the options seems to be a poor choice; it appears that we should instead listen to people who say it's clear and obvious to them, and they know exactly what we need to do *now*. Because under those circumstances, we don't want someone who cares about details; we don't care if they get the details wrong. They have the big picture right—we're good, and they're bad—and that's all the "truth" we need. We need someone who is *authentically* one of us, who is passionately loyal to us. And one way to demonstrate loyalty is to say things that are completely overstated and absurd; in such circumstances, a person who says obviously false and absurd things but who seems to be *really* one of us is exactly the person we need.

Throughout, I've talked about the tendency in demagoguery to reduce issues to "us" and "them," but I want to clarify that there might be multiple "thems." Even at its height, demagoguery often posits two out-groups. One of them is cunning and completely villainous in intent. The other is animalistic, stupid, prone to following, and possibly duped by the cunning villain, but also capable of childlike submissiveness. Demagoguery relies heavily on metaphors of vermin, disease, taint, queerness (that is, transgressive behavior), monstrosity (what is sometimes called "hybridity"–things that combine two supposedly discrete categories, such as women who are authorities, liberal Christians, Republicans opposed to the Iraq invasion), disorder, lack of control (licentiousness), thinking (rather than doing), femininity, and demonic possession for that first kind of *them*. It associates dithering, wavering, impaired masculinity, and weakness with that second kind of *them*. It associates purity, tumescence (think rigidity in the face of flaccid opposition), masculinity, order, action, decisiveness, and control with *us*.

V.
Demagoguery: A Case Study

In the spring of 1942, Americans were facing considerable uncertainty and anxiety. The war in the Pacific was not going well, and Japan had been more successful than expected. Official reports made it clear that the attack on Pearl Harbor was made possible not by sabotage but by poor decisions and errors on the part of the American military. *We* had made mistakes. In the midst of that anxiety, and after years of anti-Japanese demagoguery, the question arose as to what to do with people living in the United States who were citizens of the countries with whom we were at war. That question subtly morphed into the question of what to do with anyone of

Japanese ancestry, whether they were American or not.

During this uncertainty, California congressman John Tolan had a series of hearings about what should be done with citizens of Germany, Italy, and Japan who were living in the United States. Earl Warren was then attorney general for the state of California, and he testified to the effect that "the Japanese" (a term he never defined) were, in fact, inherently dangerous and plotting sabotage.

Warren's argument bore all the hallmarks of demagoguery. He offered his listeners security from invasion or attack, presented his case as certain, blamed the country's ill (vaguely defined as military insecurity and fear) on "the Japanese," and evaded the rhetorical responsibilities such as participating thoroughly in the hearings by listening to the experts who disagreed with him. He assumed a binary between "Japanese" and "American," while actually discussing American citizens of Japanese ethnicity—an identity that collapses the binary. The bulk of his testimony was shoddy evidence that supposedly showed they (in this case "the Japanese") were inherently disloyal with essentially and unchangeably bad motives.

His main argument was that "the Japanese" were about to engage in a level and kind of sabotage that would "mean disaster both to California and our Nation."* He had four ways he tried to support that claim. First, he asked a lot of police and peace officers of various kinds whether they thought the Japanese were trustworthy, and he repeated their opinions as though they constituted obvious proof. Second, he presented maps that showed that people of Japanese ancestry owned land near places that could be sabotaged, such as factories, ports, water plants, railroads, highways, power lines, radio stations, and so on, thereby violating fairness rules (he didn't generate such maps for

---

* US Congress, House, Select Committee Investigating National Defense Migration, *National Defense Migration Hearings.* 77th Cong., 2nd sess. (Washington, DC: Government Printing Office, 1942), 11012.

Italians or Germans) and indulging in motivism, since he assumed, without any evidence, that they had bad motives for such land ownership. Third, he said that he had been told that "the Japanese" never inform on other Japanese, whereas Italians and Germans do—a claim he never investigated (an argument from personal conviction that he never tested). Fourth, while insisting that sabotage had factored into the success of the Japanese attack on Pearl Harbor (it hadn't), he also insisted that the lack of sabotage in California was proof that sabotage was imminent (there was, he said, an "invisible deadline"),* a way of arguing that makes his entire case impervious to disproof.

Warren's maps showed that people of Japanese ethnicity owned lands where everyone else did—near roads, harbors, water sources. If owning land near accoutrements of civilization is proof of villainy, then everyone's a villain. But that wasn't his claim. Instead,

---

* Ibid.

his "proof" pointed only to *Japanese* villainy because he was looking for proof of their villainy. Warren asked himself how things would look if he was right; he didn't ask himself what land ownership would have looked like if the Japanese were innocent. It would have looked exactly the way it did. His argument wasn't falsifiable.

That is, he showed that areas with high population will be denser near infrastructure—railroads, ports, water sources, power lines. Aristotle pointed out that in political arguments we tend to rely on "enthymemes" (essentially, compressed syllogisms). Warren's enthymeme would be something like: "The Japanese are evil because they own land near important sites." That enthymeme has what scholars of argument call a "major premise"—that people who own land near important sites are evil.* But,

---

* A major premise is a claim that is unstated but logically assumed by an argument. So, for instance, "Chester hates cats because Chester is a dog" logically assumes that all dogs hate cats. If, as is the case, not all dogs hate cats, then the major premise is flawed.

obviously, he didn't believe that—it's an absurd premise. Warren wouldn't have accepted that as a good argument for incarcerating everyone who owned land near power lines, after all. Warren went looking for evidence to support his beliefs when he should have looked for evidence to falsify them.

Earlier, I mentioned that productive democratic deliberation requires that we take responsibility for our arguments, including for the assumptions we make. This bad enthymeme of Warren's exemplifies why that rule matters. His argument was logical only if the premise—owning land near important sites is proof of nefarious intention—was something *he* believed, and he didn't.

Another irresponsible kind of argument is the "damned if you do, damned if you don't" trap. Warren claimed that he had been told that "the Japanese" didn't inform on each other, which he took as damning proof. Tolan asked some of the witnesses who testified against imprisonment about that claim, and one of them said that it wasn't true—they did report suspicious behavior. "So there are Japanese spies?" asked one of the other congressmen. So they were damned if they did. Had there been sabotage, that would have been proof of the threat posed by "the Japanese," but, according to Warren, so was the absence of sabotage.* The argument that "the Japanese" were inherently treasonous was one that pro-internment speakers supported with claims that accounted for every contingency, and therefore couldn't be disproven—which is how demagoguery works.

And as with the land ownership argument, Warren's argument about reporting/not

---

* It's interesting that current defenders of mass incarceration make the same logical mistake when they reference Japanese internment. They argue that the lack of sabotage shows that imprisonment worked. They ignore that there also was no sabotage in Hawaii, which had a larger Japanese population than any of the western states where internment was enacted, and Hawaii never incarcerated its Japanese population.

reporting and sabotage/not sabotage wasn't used as evidence of the threat presented by Germans, even though Warren believed that German sabotage had significantly helped Nazi success in Europe. Warren, and others who argued for treating "the Japanese" differently, could mentally distinguish among kinds of Germans and Italians, and see them as an internally diverse group. He perceived "the Japanese," however, as essentially identical and prone to what we might call "hive mind."

It's important to note that Warren was refuted during the hearings, but he didn't stay around to listen. An expert on Norway pointed out that the notion of sabotage having had any impact on Nazi success was a myth. Others noted that there hadn't been sabotage at Pearl Harbor, and in response to Warren's argument that the lack of sabotage was proof that sabotage was planned, one person said, "I don't think that's real logic."

He listened to the police officers, who agreed with him, but he didn't try to talk to people who disagreed.

Warren later regretted his activism for internment (as did the United States, which eventually formally apologized). In his memoirs, he expressed deep regret for having supported internment, and he said, "Whenever I thought of the innocent little children who were torn from home, school friends, and congenial surroundings, I was conscience-stricken."* The question is, why didn't he think about those children in 1942? Had he imagined the situation from the perspective of the Japanese in 1942, he would have had to think about that—about the children, about what it would mean to them. He would also have had to think about why people buy land where they do, and far more innocent answers would have presented

---

* Earl Warren, *The Memoirs of Chief Justice Earl Warren* (Garden City: Doubleday, 1977), 149.

themselves. Had he asked himself whether his evidence would be just as compelling were it about Germans or Italians, or had he asked himself what kind of evidence would prove him wrong, his conscience might not have been so stricken later on. All of those questions were raised by other speakers— ones to whom he didn't listen. Getting past the demagoguery would have necessitated not just thinking more, or trying to be less emotional, or looking for data, but looking at things differently, and thinking about being wrong, and listening.

Warren recognized the problems with his stance when he imagined being *them*, when the very binary of "us" and "them" was transcended by his moment of compassionate imagination. I've used Warren's demagoguery as an example not only because it shows that it isn't a question of good versus bad people (he did both good and bad things in his life, like most people), but also because his support for and later regret about internment shows that the best way to open the Faraday cage* of demagoguery isn't by aspiring to some emotion-free hyper-rationalism; it's by practicing compassion for those whom demagoguery says we should treat as Other. It's by imagining things from their perspective.

---

* A Faraday cage is an enclosure that greatly restricts electromagnetic transmissions, especially incoming. There can be transmission within the enclosure, and sometimes transmission out.

VI.
A Culture of Demagoguery

Demagoguery depoliticizes politics, in that it says we don't have to argue policies, and can just rouse ourselves to new levels of commitment to *us* and purify our community or nation of *them*. It says that we are in such a desperate situation that we can no longer afford *them* the same treatment we want for *us*. But demagoguery rarely *starts* by calling for the literal extermination of the out-group.*

---

* Adolf Hitler's March 23, 1933, speech before the Reichstag, in which he announced his plans for his new administration, never mentions either exterminating various groups or starting another war. In fact, all his speeches prior to the moment of invading Poland were about his desire for peace, and his public speeches relied on dog whistles about racial purity.

Demagoguery isn't a disease or infection; it's more like algae in a pond. Algae can be benign—in small amounts, even helpful. But if the conditions of the pond are such that the algae begins to crowd out other kinds of pond life and ecological processes, then it creates an environment in which nothing but algae can thrive, and so more algae leads to yet more. That's what demagoguery can do, create an environment of more and more demagoguery. Then, for people competing for media markets, consumers, voters, and so on, demagoguery is likely to be the more effective rhetorical strategy, and more rhetors will choose it. And rhetors have to out-demagogue each other to get attention, buyers, voters.

Weimar Germany (the world in which the Nazis rose) had a lot of problems—intermittently high inflation, high unemployment, a highly factionalized media (much of which promoted racist conspiracy theories), and a government hamstrung by political parties that, making a virtue of fanatical commitment to purity, demonized the normal politics of compromise, deliberation, and argumentation. Those were serious problems, and none of them were going to go away on their own. It's generally argued that World War I was a consequence of nationalism, militarism, and wishful thinking. There were, therefore, multiple causes of Germany's woes—but Hitler never talked about those causes. Instead of trying to reduce factionalism, nationalism, militarism, and wishful thinking, or come up with economic solutions, Hitler argued that all of Germany's problems, especially its having lost the war, but including its current economic ones, could be traced to two *real* problems: a weakness of will and the presence of alien bodies. Germany needed, he said, *more* fanatical factionalism, nationalism, militarism, and wishful thinking, which it could achieve by purifying itself of *them*.

He wasn't the only one to blame Germany's problems on *them*, although there was some disagreement as to who *they* were. For the Bolsheviks it was capitalists and liberals; for fascists it was Bolsheviks (who were mysteriously interchangeable with Jews) and liberals; for many Christians the problem was the Jews; for others it was union leaders; and the Sinti and Roma were commonly characterized as degraded and criminal. There wasn't much agreement in Weimar political discourse, but there was nearly perfect agreement that the problem was the presence of a bad sort of person. The "ill" part of the policy argument was truncated to *them*. Hitler may be the most famous example of a German rhetor who engaged in this kind of demagoguery, but he didn't invent it.

This kind of rhetoric is the first step on what the sociologist Michael Mann has identified as a journey that can end in genocide, classicide, or politicide—that is, mass murder on the basis of race, class, or ideology. I envision this journey more as a ladder, because each step to a higher rung raises the risk of harm (not just to democracy but physical harm, too). But it's important to remember that communities that reach that final rung rarely start out with an explicitly exterminationist political agenda. Instead, they start out with a world in which "the ill" is reduced to the presence of some infecting group, and this reduction doesn't happen as the consequence of one rhetorical magician waving a word-wand. It happens because a lot of people are making that kind of argument. Hitler couldn't have come to power, let alone tame the Reichstag, hogtie the dissenting press, and hamstring the judiciary, if Weimar Germany hadn't been a culture of demagoguery.

The lowest rung on the ladder is simply a lot of "us versus them" rhetoric, and multiple groups might be engaged in it with each other. After all, in Weimar Germany, Nazis weren't the only anti-Semitic, Aryanist nationalist group. Soviet-supported communist groups (not all communist groups were Soviet-supported) similarly said it was an absolutely stark choice between them and everyone else, and they famously refused to compromise with "liberal" or "moderate" groups. During segregation in the United States, numerous states had laws grounded in what "whites" versus "coloreds" could do, not just Southern states. In the 1960s, while the radical right-wing group the John Birch Society called everyone to its left "communist," the radical left-wing group the Weathermen called everyone to its right "fascist." Right now, the GOP is engulfed in an argument about who is or is not a RINO (Republican in Name Only), and the Dems seem poised to engage in exactly the kind of purity war that has never served them well.

If everyone agrees that demagoguery is bad, and if there is good evidence that it pushes communities in a direction that can end in genocide, why does anyone engage in it? Why do we climb that ladder? There are various contributing factors, especially when large numbers of voters get all their information from partisan sources that profit from demagoguery. Equally important is how a culture imagines public discourse. Demagoguery thrives when a culture imagines all political argument in any of these three ways (or some combination of them): as an antagonistic contest in which crushing or silencing the other side is victory, as merely about expressing your point of view, or as bargaining. In rhetorical terms, demagoguery is the consequence of seeing public discourse as exclusively compliance-gaining, expressive, or bargaining.

In compliance-gaining situations, everyone in the discussion is determined to win, and they will say whatever they need to in order to do so. The point of such public discourse is not to find the best solution to a community's problems, but to triumph over the other side. That triumph might happen because you've gotten large numbers of people to agree with you, or because you've intimidated dissenters into silence. In any case, there are no rhetorical strategies off the table—dishonesty, threats, fallacies, and anything else are all fine if they lead to your group's success. Rhetorical might makes right, and the ends (success) justify the means. Changing your mind, in this world, is a loss, and to be avoided (or denied) at all costs.

Demagoguery also thrives in an expressive public sphere. That is one in which people simply express their own opinions, without engaging anyone else's argument. It can be an expressive sphere in which niceness is valued, such as an adult Sunday school class in which it would be considered rude to disagree with what someone else says. You can also have expressive and antagonistic arenas, such as a sporting event at which fans shout at each other during the game. The latter is especially friendly to demagoguery because, in that world, no one is expected to make actual arguments (with evidence and credible sources), nor to represent fairly the claims of the other side. It would be bizarre for someone to hold up a sign that carefully refutes a YOUR TEAM SUCKS poster being held by someone on the other side. If we treat politics as a zero-sum game between us and them, then the kind of compassionate imagination that enabled Warren to recognize his error is actively prohibited—you aren't supposed to want a game in which everyone wins, or to bemoan bad calls that help you.

Demagoguery can help in a bargaining situation, too, but it can have some rhetorical blowback. In a bargaining situation, power comes from posing a bigger plausible threat (if you don't get your way, you will do *this*). A particularly effective position of power is to be someone who is barely controlling a passionate, reckless, and potentially violent crowd—of course, it's a plausible threat only if there really is such a crowd. Thus, to make this threat work, you must have roused a crowd to the point of violence, on the grounds that you must get your way in your negotiations, completely and entirely, or they are in danger of extermination. And in a bargaining situation, the best way to get what you really want is to begin by overstating your demands, so you have to have roused your base to the point that they will accept nothing less than something more extreme than you really think you need.

And then you succeed, and you get what you really think you need. What will you tell your base now that you have to persuade them to accept a position you previously insisted was not nearly enough? If you've previously insisted that compromise was suicidal, you look as though you've thrown them to the wolves. If you look as though your hyperbole was rhetorically cunning, you can look inauthentic. You've now made yourself vulnerable to someone else who might want to co-opt that base by promising the base to get more than you did, and so the demagoguery goes up a rung.*

---

* Thus, there's always a little bit of demagoguery in a situation that relies on bargaining. If public discourse is always and only bargaining, then the culture will have a lot of demagoguery.

Hence, this slouching up the ladder is an odd way that demagoguery entraps the rhetors who try to use it. Once they have convinced their followers (or viewers) that it's kill or be killed, any policy short of complete purification makes no sense, and it's difficult to argue that normal politics is adequate. That is, *they* are no longer simply irritating, but incessantly and inevitably plotting the extermination of *us*. Therefore, we are justified in attacking, expelling, and even exterminating them—it's necessary self-defense. In such a situation, extraordinary action is called for—you can't compromise about your own extermination.

Unhappily, when demagoguery is the norm, it traps all politicians, in that if you don't say *they* are the worst ever, you are obviously an idiot, or in their pay. Television programs that offer nuanced analyses can't compete with programs that simultaneously enrage and please; talk radio that is fair to all positions is too cognitively complex to be engaging; and print or online media that says *they* might have a point is frustrating.

Scholars of media and communication describe much of our current media as "infotainment"—it looks as if it's informing the audience, but the real goal is entertainment that will improve ratings. When it's for profit, then the goal is also to hold on to an audience, which necessarily means trying to persuade the audience that they don't need to look at other sources. Thus, the very nature of much of our media is to try to create informational enclaves. This isn't a new phenomenon—one of many striking features of the antebellum culture was the rabidly factionalized media. And that factionalized media enabled the construction of a world of "alternative facts" in which all abolitionists were motivated by jealousy that they couldn't own slaves, a desire to sleep with slaves, and an active desire for the race war they were continually advocating—positions that couldn't have been seriously maintained by anyone who read the abolitionists' literature. By the time of the Civil War, large numbers of Southerners were certain that Lincoln planned to use his power to force abolition on the South, which would be enforced by his use of federal troops. In fact, he was willing to sign a constitutional amendment that would have protected slavery in the states where it existed, and he didn't have enough support in Congress to get a federal-level emancipation act passed. But I don't think many people in slave states knew that, since Southern newspapers never mentioned it. Media—magazines, books, speeches, sermons, even novels—aimed to give people talking points that would resolve the cognitive dissonance created by the pro-slavery policy agenda, and they succeeded. The consequence was that pro-slavery rhetoric seemed to create a very strange world which its ideal consumers completely inhabited.

These media also did something that was named only in the mid-twentieth century (in a panic over supposed "brainwashing" of

American soldiers in Korea): They inoculated their readers against significant criticism of slavery by presenting them with weak versions of it, just as you can make people more resistant to smallpox by exposing them to cowpox. Demagogic media presents its consumers with dumbed-down (or even completely fabricated) versions of opposition arguments. Consumers of such media sincerely believe they already know what *they* think, and therefore don't need to look at original sources, dissenting points of view, or any evidence *they* might try to present.

It wasn't just that the media was thoroughly factionalized, but that the factionalized media successfully created an alternative world. Pro-slavery rhetors could refer to events that never happened (such as various fantastical abolitionist conspiracies) or events that didn't happen in the way they were described (such as South Carolina's supposedly having triumphed in the Nullification Crisis—it was trounced) and count on their audience accepting the premises. It was an alternative world, and it was shared. That was specifically what I also saw in 2003 public discourse about the Iraq invasion—media puddles that had no contact with other systems, and it's gotten worse since. We are a nation divided by media.

VII.
What Do We Do?

Here's what we don't do. Demagoguery says that all of our problems can be solved if we purify our group of the bad people who are causing the problems. So, we don't try to solve the problem of demagoguery by purifying our community of *this* demagogue or *his* followers. Not only is that a demagogic solution, but it won't even solve the problem. Unless we change the culture, we'll just get another demagogue.

Demagoguery says the solution is simple. It would be actively bizarre for me to have spent all this time talking about the complexities of demagoguery and then propose a simple solution. Were the solution simple, then demagoguery would have died when Thucydides, a fifth-century BCE historian, slammed the notorious demagogue Cleon, and Aristotle would have included in his fourth-century book on rhetoric a list of how to stop it. It isn't simple.

There are, loosely, four kinds of things we can do, and no one needs to do all of them, and none of us needs to do any of them all the time. First, we can try to reduce the profitability of demagoguery by consuming less of it ourselves, and shaming media outlets that rely heavily on it. Second, we can choose not to argue with family or friends who are repeating demagogic talking points, and simply give witness to the benefits of pluralism and diversity. Or, third, if it seems interesting and worthwhile, we can argue with family or friends who are repeating demagogic talking points. Fourth, we can also support and argue for democratic deliberation.

Historically, cultures insist on non-demagogic political processes after a devastating war (consider the rise of arguments for religious tolerance after the English Civil Wars or the marginalization of racialist "science" after World War II). It would be nice if we could find a different solution.

Demagoguery is powerfully reduced when it stops getting people elected, and that usually happens because of in-group policing. Similarly, when it isn't profitable for a media outlet to engage in demagoguery, it won't, and that happens when its target market declines to put up with it. Individual demagogues are best stopped by in-group condemnation, and particular strains of demagoguery are generally ended by public shaming. There are complicated issues about the kind of deliberately marginalized demagoguery that profits or succeeds by being seen as counterculture, but that's a different book (it's the "should you punch a Nazi" debate, and it's vexed).

In *Phaedrus*, Socrates says that writing is like throwing a seed over a wall. That statement is often taken as a condemnation of writing, but Plato *wrote* it, and he was no dummy. He was making the point that persuasion doesn't necessarily happen instantly, and we can't always know in the moment whether we have succeeded. Arguing with people (or not arguing, and simply telling stories) is like throwing seeds over a wall. I've argued tooth and nail with people who insisted I was wrong whom I later saw abandon their earlier position and adopt mine, all the while insisting I had not persuaded them. I have also seen people reargue the same point over and over, despite getting rhetorically pantsed on it. My whole career has been about trying to figure out how to persuade people to engage in deliberation, and I've been off and on arguing in the world of digitally connected discourse since the mid-1980s; I taught debate, I teach argumentation, and even I feel that I've only started to develop useful strategies in the last three years or so. And those strategies don't always work. Many people prefer a comfortable lie to an uncomfortable truth, so the task isn't easy.

But as mentioned above, there are four strategies that might help correct our course.

1) We can work to reduce the profitability of demagoguery by consuming less of it ourselves, and shaming media outlets that rely heavily on it.

American political discourse should have a lower ratio of demagoguery to inclusive argumentation, but that doesn't mean we should never consume demagoguery. Consuming demagoguery is like lying on a couch watching bad movies—there's no harm in doing it from time to time, especially if we also get up and move around. But we should spend some time out of our own informational enclaves. We should make sure we are reading multiple points of view, especially some with which we disagree vehemently. We should try to listen to the views we find abhorrent and try to be able to summarize them in ways that are accurate. We don't do these things in order to find common ground, or discover that they aren't so bad, but because it's important to understand *why* people find demagoguery attractive. And if you do choose to argue with them, you'll be able to show that you know what they believe—you won't be relying on a garbled secondhand version of it. Indulging in some in-group demagoguery is fine, and may even be necessary for recharging, but it shouldn't be our only or main source of information.

Further, we should not ignore the power of boycotts, and the pressure that can be put on advertisers. We shouldn't be trying to silence views simply because we disagree with them, although it's fair to take issue with *how* those views are presented. If a political agenda cannot be explained and defended in a non-demagogic way, then that's a serious problem, and it's an important point. If a media outlet engages exclusively or primarily in demagoguery, then it's fair to ask it to change.

2) We can choose to try to persuade people who are repeating demagogic talking points while choosing not to get into arguments with them.

Demagoguery about *them* is undone by empathy. Generalizations about *them* are complicated, and sometimes shattered, by experiences with individual members of *them*, or even humanizing stories. Tell those stories, mention those friends, talk about those experiences, and just refuse to argue. Invite your interlocutor to meet *them*, point out the individuals who don't fit the stereotype, and, if you are a member of their outgroup, then resist your interlocutor's desire to treat you as an exception. Many of the people who explain how they came to reject demagoguery about some out-group say they were changed when they got to know (and love) people in that group, or when they discovered that people whom they had long loved were members of the out-group. Just bear witness to the glory of diversity and pluralism.

There are some people who argue that humor can work, since demagoguery takes itself very seriously. Demagogic humor is generally mean, and doesn't have the destabilizing effect that a lot of humor has (in which at least part of the joke is on the person telling it)—it's only about the out-group and their minions. I don't think that kind of humor works effectively at undermining faith in demagoguery or its specific claims because it confirms demagoguery's premise that the in-group is being victimized. Instead, the kind of humor that operates on the premise that demagoguery is often very silly in its claims is more likely to work. Making fun of demagogic hyperbolic and apocalyptic predictions, for instance, especially the ones to which they once committed themselves (remember the way that all those falsified predictions about Obama taking our guns in 2008 had no impact on people making exactly the same argument in 2012) can be effective. Personally, I'm not usually comfortable with this strategy myself, but I have to admit that historically it's been powerful, as in the "God hates figs" response to various homophobic groups.*

3) Or, you might choose to argue with family, friends, or random people who are repeating demagogic talking points.†

This strategy is probably the most complicated, and impossible to explain briefly. So what follows isn't really a how-to—it takes people years to learn to argue effectively, and therefore a few

---

* When homophobic rhetoric became associated with signs saying GOD HATES FAGS, many counter-protesters responded with signs saying GOD HATES FIGS (a play on Matthew 21:9), or GOD HATES CORDUROY (a play on Leviticus 19:19).

† One of those random people might be yourself. This can be difficult to recognize when we are in an enclave of demagoguery—since we hear certain claims again and again, they seem normal and reasonable. We might be able to identify only demagoguery with which we disagree. The most straightforward way to determine if *we* are basing our beliefs on demagoguery is to apply these strategies to our own beliefs—for instance, would we have the same reaction to this kind of argument if the out-group made it?

pages in a book can offer only a set of pointers. In that spirit, here are some pointers.

You can argue with others compassionately and kindly, or not—with some people the kindness strategy works. The compassionate version can involve being curious about their positions, including being curious about the contradictions, or it can involve a lot of establishing common ground. Both of those strategies work best when they're sincere—when you really are curious, and you really do have a lot of common ground. It also requires that the people you're talking with are sincere, that they are open to new ideas, care about being consistent, and care more about finding what's true than being right. With some people (those who like demagoguery because of its dominance or oppositional stance) an aggressive and confrontational strategy works better.

But, with either kind of person, what will you argue about? Here the concept of stases is tremendously useful—and, basically, if you can keep an eye on the stasis of an argument, you can "win" an argument with someone engaged in demagoguery (whether that will persuade that person or anyone watching is a different story).

Demagoguery works by shifting the stasis to group identity, and it can happen by insisting that you are an out-group member for making your argument, your sources are out-group, or you're duped by the out-group. Resist the shift to identity (unless you're going to make the argument that they are dishonoring their in-group—a complicated strategy described below). The first step is to resist the "your argument can be dismissed because it's an out-group argument" stasis shift; if you do nothing but persuade someone (the person with whom you're arguing or the observers) that that is the stasis on which your interlocutor is arguing, that's an achievement. If you can get them to admit that there might be other stases, then you can try to move to more productive stases, such as accuracy of claims, credibility of sources, internal consistency in arguments, or fairness.

Demagoguery will generally consist of claims ("alternative facts") that are perceived as true by the targeted audience because they confirm previously held beliefs, and *one stasis is to refute the claims.* You can refute them with credible sources (e.g., ones that link to primary documents), but you'll end up in the bias argument unless you use sources from their in-group. So, either be prepared to have the argument about bias and sources or, if you can, use in-group sources or primary documents to show their claims are untrue (it's often surprisingly easy). You can also insist that they give a source. If they do (they generally won't), you will often find the source does not actually support their claim (the headline does), or that the source both supports and refutes the claim, or it's a fake news site. People who believe in naïve realism don't necessarily feel the need to click on links—the headline is enough—so they can be usefully flummoxed by quoting from the article they've cited. You don't have to rely on "libtard" sources of lists of fake news sites—a couple of minutes on a site will usually turn up the disclaimer (this is for entertainment, or this is satire) that will enable you to show it's a fake news site.

Because the practice of inoculation (mentioned earlier) persuades people that they always already know what the out-group is arguing, you can spend a lot of time trying to get someone to stay on the stasis of *this* argument, and it's important that you do so. If, for instance, everything you've read in your informational enclave says that all squirrel supporters also believe that kicking puppies is good, and you're arguing with someone who says that squirrels have some good qualities, you might be tempted to attack them for kicking puppies. That stasis shift would seem reasonable to you, but it has two leaps in it, either of which might be unmerited. You're assuming that they *support* squirrels, and perhaps they just think squirrels aren't entirely bad. You're also assuming that all squirrel supporters are alike and necessarily advocate puppy kicking. You may find yourself on the other side of that move, with someone attacking you for positions their information sources have said people like you always have. In both cases, it's helpful to try to make sure you are both arguing with what real people really believe, and not with straw men, before you shift the stasis from squirrel supporting to puppy kicking.

For many people, politics is a zero-sum game, rather than the realm in which, together, we find solutions to our mutual problems. For such people, the *real* issue is which group is better. Therefore, if you point out a problem with something one of their political figures has done, they're very likely to respond with, "Your group does bad things too." Resist the desire to say "two wrongs don't make a right" (they think it does) and instead point out that the stasis has shifted to which group is better in some abstract way. If your point is that their figure has lied about something, it doesn't matter if your figure kicks puppies or chews broken glass by the light of the full moon—that doesn't make what their figure said true.

If they refuse to give a source, then you're in the more complicated, but, really, more important, stasis in which you *point out problems with how they're arguing*. Ultimately, your goal is simply to get people to see that the argument is demagoguery. Demagoguery pretends to be about principle ("executive orders are an outrageous violation of the Constitution") but it's about in-group versus out-group ("unless they're done by *my* president"). So, pointing out that there aren't principles involved—they object only when the other side uses executive orders, or smears, or relies on biased sources—is useful for the argument about argument. In my experience, the response is that principles don't apply to all groups because one group is inherently and essentially evil (namely, yours), so it's unlikely that you'll persuade someone that they're wrong to object to out-group executive orders, but you might plant a seed in their minds (or the minds of observers) that their beliefs are about in-group versus out-group and not principle. And, further, that they are rejecting the principle of "do unto others as you would have them do unto you," even rhetorically: They can't live by the rhetorical or logical rules to which they want to hold *others*.

You can also pursue the question of fairness in conjunction with the falsifiability question (aka "the Thanksgiving dinner argument," named for the classic scene where relatives are keen to raise political issues about which they've formed rigid, unpersuadable views). It's useful to try to infer (or simply ask) if the people with whom you're arguing are really open to argument—what are the circumstances under which they would change their mind? What are the discourse rules, and who gets to set them? If there are no circumstances under which they would change their mind, and if the rules don't apply equally to everyone at the table, then you can refuse to have the argument. (If you want to be snarky, you can do so while pointing out that it's because they can't defend their positions through a reasonable argument, but that rarely goes well.)

If you choose to argue with people about how they're arguing, you'll find yourself talking about fallacious arguments, and being able to name the fallacy is very helpful. For purposes of refuting demagogic talking points, here is a set of fallacies useful to be able to recognize.

Appealing to Inconsistent Premises: This comes about when you have at least two enthymemes, and their major premises contradict. For instance, someone might argue: "Your president is a tyrant because she issued executive orders" and "My president is decisive because he issued a lot of executive orders." Those two arguments contradict each other—if issuing a lot of EOs is tyrannical, then their president is a tyrant; if it's decisive, then your president is decisive. The person needs to be consistent as to whether issuing EOs is good or bad.

Circular Reasoning: This is another fallacy that comes about because of glitches in the relationship of claims (aka "begging the question"). This is a very common fallacy, but surprisingly difficult for people to recognize. It looks like an argument, but it is really just an assertion of the conclusion over and over again in different language. The "evidence" for the conclusion is actually the conclusion in synonyms, or the evidence is valid only if the conclusion is true. Warren's maps about land ownership are relevant to the issue only if his conclusion (they have nefarious motives) is true, but they were supposed to lead to that conclusion, not derive from it.

Genus–Species Errors: This fallacy (aka over-generalizing, ignoring exceptions, stereotyping) happens when hidden in the argument (often in the major premise) is a slip from a qualifying word such as "some," "many," "often," "sometimes," or "rarely" to absolutes such as "all," "none," "always," "never." This substitution can come from assuming that what is true of a specific thing is true of every member of that genus (all dogs hate cats because this dog hates cats), or what is true of the genus is true of every individual member of that genus (this dog must have four legs because dogs have four legs). We're all prone to this error with an out-group, since we tend to think they're all interchangeable, and so we will take a single example of an out-group member as proof that they are all bad, or a single example of a good deed on the part of an in-group hero to dismiss all criticism.

False dilemma (aka poisoning the wells, false binary, either/or) occurs when a rhetor sets out a limited number of options, generally forcing one's hand by forcing one to choose the option he or she wants. Were all the options laid out, then the situation would be more complicated, and the rhetor's proposal might not look so good. It's often an instance of scare tactics because the other option is typically a disaster (we imprison either all "the Japanese" or we'll be invaded by Japan). It is "straw man" when it's achieved by dumbing down the opponent's proposal. It can be cunning, as when a rhetor is trying to obscure the various reasonable options (salespeople will often do this), but it can be unintentional, as when someone believes that all issues can be framed as a binary.

Misuse of statistics is self-explanatory. It surprises me how often demagoguery uses bad "science" and bad statistics. People are often persuaded by the presence of footnotes, for instance, that the claims must be true (even if the footnotes are bad or irrelevant), and some irreproducibly bad statistics take on a life of their own (such as the entirely fabricated statistic that homosexuals are twelve times more likely to molest children). Showing someone why their statistics are bad, however, can be very complicated. Typically, people confuse absolute numbers with ratio—Warren's statistics about land ownership looked big because he didn't look at ownership rates. He showed that "the Japanese" owned a lot of land near infrastructure, but generally there is denser population near infrastructure. Statistics about terrorist attacks typically leave out terrorism committed by white US citizens, and often use odd definitions of "terrorist" and "terrorism." Naïve realists often believe that they can judge the validity of statistics on the basis of whether they support a conclusion they believe to be obviously true, so they accept as true those statistics with which they agree and dismiss as untrue those statistics with which they disagree.

The post hoc ergo propter hoc fallacy (aka confusing causation and correlation) is especially common in the use of social science research in policy arguments. If two things are correlated (that is, exist together) that does not necessarily mean that you can be certain which one caused the other, or whether they were both caused by something else. It generally arises in situations when people have failed to have a "control" group in a study. We often reason this way because of two dramatic events that happened in sequence; our tendency to assume they must be connected is an instance of the cognitive bias to see patterns. This fallacy is a major factor in the demagoguery about vaccines.

Fallacies of Relevance: Really, all of the remaining fallacies in this section could be grouped under *red herring*, which consists of dragging something so stinky across the trail of an argument that people take the wrong track. Also called "shifting the stasis," it's trying to distract from what is really at stake between two people to something else—usually inflammatory, but sometimes simply easier ground for the person engaged in the red herring.

Ad hominem is an irrelevant attack on the identity of an interlocutor. Dismissing someone's argument because their having made that argument shows them to be a "libtard," "neoliberal stooge," "neocon fascist" or some other out-group is generally ad hominem—it's saying, "Your argument is wrong because you are out-group." Not all "attacks" on a person or their character are ad hominem. Accusing someone of being dishonest, making a bad argument, or engaging in fallacies is not ad hominem because it's attacking their argument. Even attacking the person ("you are a liar") is not fallacious if it's relevant and supported with evidence.

Ad verecundiam is the term for a fallacious appeal to authority. This fallacy is very common in demagoguery, since in-group membership is often taken as ensuring credibility. Sometimes the authority has vague credentials ("a scientist"), and sometimes irrelevant (a PhD in mechanical engineering does not make someone an expert on global warming). Warren's reliance on police and peace officers is an example of a fallacious appeal to authority: Even if they were very good at their jobs, they had neither training nor expertise in identifying spies. Appeal to personal conviction is generally an example of this fallacy.*

Ad misericordiam is the term for an irrelevant appeal to emotion, such as saying you should vote for me because I have the most adorable dogs (even though I really

---

* There's nothing inherently fallacious about appeal to authority, but having a good conversation might mean that the relevance of the authority and their expertise now has to become the stasis.

do). In demagoguery, there is often an appeal to fear in that the situation is supposed to be so dire that we cannot even afford to argue—thus, it's an attempt to silence disagreement. Often, the fear that some people feel is supposed to be proof of the identity, motives, or actions of others, and it may not be. For instance, the fear to which Warren pointed as evidence of the impending treachery of "the Japanese" wasn't actually evidence of anything about people of Japanese ethnicity; it was just evidence of racism. Emotions are always part of reasoning, so merely appealing to emotions is not necessarily fallacious; people who refuted Warren also appealed to feelings, such as feelings of compassion, fear about the consequences for our country if we began behaving in fascist ways, and hope for a more inclusive world. It wasn't even unreasonable for Warren to feel fear for his country, but his fear wasn't proof.

Motivism is the fallacy of rejecting someone's argument on the basis that you assume they have bad motives, when their motives are irrelevant. So, saying that you can reject a source because it's "biased," and your only evidence of "bias" is that it is an out-group source, is motivism. Motivism is often a circular argument, in the sense that it's non-falsifiable, as it was in the case of Warren.

Scare tactics (aka apocalyptic language) is a fallacy if the scary outcome is irrelevant, unlikely, or inevitable regardless of the actions. For instance, if I say you should vote for me and then give you a terrifying description of how our sun will someday go supernova, that's scare tactics (unless I'm claiming I'm going to prevent that outcome somehow). Warren's fearmongering about the "invisible deadline" exemplified this fallacy. There hadn't been sabotage in the Pearl Harbor attack, let alone on the West Coast. Japan hadn't tried to invade

Hawaii, and an invasion of the mainland was even less likely and definitely not imminent (it would have required establishing bases). If Japan did intend to invade (they didn't, as the US government knew), imprisoning everyone of Japanese ethnicity wouldn't have made any difference.

Straw man is dumbing down the opposition argument. Because the rhetor is now responding to arguments their opponent never made, most of what they have to say is irrelevant. Media inoculation is a cunning use of straw man, but people sometimes engage in this one unintentionally by not listening, projecting, and tending to assume that anyone who disagrees with them is stupid. If we are naïve realists, then we believe that our perceptions are ones shared by every reasonable person; someone who disagrees with us is unreasonable, and so we attribute unreasonable views to them. People who engage in binary thinking tend to assume that something either never happens or always does, and they also tend to hear others' claims in such either/or terms, so they unintentionally attribute all-or-nothing claims to others. Thus, if I say that there was no sabotage in Pearl Harbor, a person who relies on binary thinking might believe that I've said there was no sabotage in the United States during World War II. If I believe that anyone who disagrees with me about gun ownership and sales wants to ban all guns, then I might respond to your argument about requiring gun safes with something about the government kicking through our doors and taking all of our guns (an example of slippery slope).

Tu quoque is usually (but not always) a kind of red herring, but sometimes it's the **fallacy of false equivalence** (what George Orwell called the notion that half a loaf is no better than none). One argues that "you did it too!" This fallacy is very common in demagoguery because of the underlying assumption that all public policy issues can be settled by determining which group is better. For instance, if I say that your candidate shouldn't be trusted in his claims about being honest because he embezzled a million dollars, and you respond by saying my candidate didn't try to give back extra change from a vending machine, that would be the fallacy of false equivalence. If you respond by saying that I once didn't try to give back extra change from a vending machine, that would be tu quoque.

~

For reasons unclear even to me, being able to name the fallacy has significant rhetorical power in arguments with people persuaded by demagoguery, and so it's useful. But being able to fallacy-shame people isn't sufficient. Basically, we need to persuade people to engage in more deliberation and less demagoguery. That isn't easy because demagoguery isn't just a way of arguing about politics; it's a way of thinking about decision-making.

Demagoguery is the reduction of politics to in-group versus out-group, with the assumption and claim that the in-group is always and forever and in every way better than the out-group. Oddly enough, that premise can present an opportunity for persuading someone to stop repeating talking points uncritically. Pointing out that the stereotype about their group is that they can't argue without resorting to insult, and can't support their point with internally consistent arguments, can set them up for having to prove their rhetorical honor. One of the paradoxes about demagoguery is that it is simultaneously shameless and obsessed with honor. Shaming them about being internally inconsistent, incapable of reasonable defenses, citing sources that actually contradict what they say—that puts front and center the cognitive dissonance between their shamelessness and their obsession with honor.

None of these strategies work with people who are deep into conspiracy theories, nor with bots, nor with people paid to argue, but, at least in a public forum, pointing out what is happening can get some other people to walk away from demagoguery. Notice that I'm not saying you will thereby persuade them they are wrong. After all, they might not be. You might be wrong. You might both be wrong. You might both be somewhat right. You're trying to persuade them to engage in deliberation, and that means you have to be willing to engage in it, too.

4) Hence, the most important tactic is to support and argue for democratic deliberation.

In other words, channel Thucydides. Thucydides wrote about the Peloponnesian War with Sparta, the one that tanked the Athenian Empire. Thucydides described in some detail a debate between two speakers, Cleon and

Diodotus, about whether to commit genocide of the Mytileneans, some of whom had tried to rebel against their alliance with Athens. Cleon gives a completely demagogic speech about how deliberation is unnecessary, anyone who disagrees with him is corrupt, and the Athenians should wipe out Mytilene just to terrorize everyone else. Diodotus (perhaps an invention of Thucydides') makes a passionate argument for argumentation. He says that we should think about policies in terms of their long-term effectiveness, not just whether they please some desire for revenge; that disagreement is good; and that we have to have a world in which dissent is okay. Thucydides asked that his audience think about *how* we argue, not just *what* we argue.

And this brings us back to the question of democratic deliberation. Earlier, I mentioned concepts particularly helpful for democratic deliberation: inclusion, fairness, responsibility, self-skepticism, and the "stases." Those can be turned into four basic principles.

First, because demagoguery depends on *us* and *them* being treated differently, simply insisting on fairness can go a long way toward undermining demagoguery. Rhetorical fairness means that, whatever the argument rules are, they apply equally to everyone in the argument. So, if a kind of argument is deemed "rational" for the in-group, then it's just as "rational" for the out-group (e.g., if a single personal experience counts as proof for a claim, then a single appeal to personal experience suffices to disprove that claim; personal attack is acceptable or prohibited for all participants; and so on). Second, fairness connects to responsibility in that the responsibilities of argumentation should apply equally across interlocutors, so that all parties are responsible for representing one another's arguments fairly, and striving to provide internally consistent evidence to support their claims. Third, the people arguing should strive to be internally consistent in terms of appeals to premises, definitions, and standards. Or, to put it in the negative, the claims of an argument shouldn't contradict each other or appeal to contradictory premises; if something is defined one way at one point in the argument, it isn't defined in an opposite way elsewhere; if something is described as good at one point, it isn't bad in another; and if there are inconsistencies (which might be valid), then the person accused of making them takes responsibility for them and for trying to explain them. Finally, the issue is actually up for *argument*—that is, the people involved are making claims that can be proven wrong, and that they can imagine abandoning, modifying, and reconsidering.

These aren't rules that enable someone to referee an argument the way one can ref a football game—it's all up for argument. If one person thinks someone else has violated one of the rules, then *that* becomes the stasis of the argument. These aren't rules that enable certainty; they are rules that help us navigate uncertainty. They are rules that invite us to argue *with* one another, rather than express nasty thoughts about them. We don't always have to behave this way in discourse, and there can be a lot of fun in pursuing an argument with someone even if neither of us will change our minds, but we aren't in the realm of democratic deliberation.

~

Good disagreements are the bedrock of communities. Good disagreements happen when people with different kinds of expertise and points of view talk and listen to one another, and when we try, honestly and pragmatically, to determine the best course of action for our whole community. Our differences make our decisions stronger. Democracy presumes that we can behave as one community, caring together for our common life, and disagreeing productively and honestly with one another. Demagoguery rejects that pragmatic acceptance and even valuing of disagreement in favor of a world of certainty, purity, and silencing of dissent.

Demagoguery is about saying *we* are never wrong; *they* are. If we made a mistake, *they* are to blame; *we* are always in touch with what is true and right. There is no such thing as a complicated problem; there are just people trying to complicate things. Even listening to *them* is a kind of betrayal. All *we* need to do is what *we* all know to be the right thing. And it's very, very pleasurable. It tells us we're good, and they're bad, that we were right all along, and that we don't need to think about things carefully or admit we're uncertain. It provides clarity.

Democracy is about disagreement, uncertainty, complexity, and making mistakes. It's about having to listen to arguments you think are obviously completely wrong; it's about being angry with other people, and their being angry with you. It's about it all taking much longer to get something passed than you think reasonable, and about taking a long time resisting some policy you think is dip-shit. Democracy is about having to listen, and compromise, and it's about being wrong (and admitting it). It's about guessing—because the world is complicated—the best course of action, and trying to look at things from various perspectives, and letting people with those various perspectives participate in the conversation.

Democracy is hard; demagoguery is easy.

Demagoguery happens because it's more pleasurable to get ourselves all worked up about some other group than it is to deliber-ate with them. Demagoguery is fun because it makes us feel really good about ourselves, it makes it seem that complicated and difficult issues are simple, and it can provide a kind of clarity. It isn't always bad, but it isn't always good. And it is bad if it's always.

Since this book's original publication, I've talked to readers and noticed some recurring questions and misunderstandings.

People often think that, since I'm condemning demagoguery, I'm advocating "civility" (which is commonly assumed to be the only other option). I'm not. As the example of Earl Warren shows, it's quite possible to come across as "civil" while still being engaged in demagoguery.

Additionally, people too often believe "civility" means a world in which we aren't angry—and certainly not angry with each other—and that's neither possible nor desirable. People who don't get angry about politics are the people who don't really care. I think we should care. I like what the political theorist Hanna Fenichel Pitkin says (in her book about Hannah Arendt, *The Attack of the Blob*) concerning what's required of people in a democracy: "the ability to fight—openly, seriously, with commitment, and about things that really matter—without fanaticism, without seeking to exterminate one's opponent."

Further, I'm not saying that all points of view are equally valid—or that both sides are just as bad. There are points of view that we can dismiss, but we shouldn't do so on the basis of what our in-group sources tell us *they,* our opponents, believe. We have to make sure we really understand out-group points of view, by trying to find the strongest arguments available to them—not the straw man arguments our factional media give us.

People sometimes ask why I picked Earl Warren as my example, or they assume I picked him because I dislike him. I chose

Warren because he engaged in what I consider a particularly pernicious kind of demagoguery. He was polite and apparently calm throughout his testimony, and he was armed with data (and a lot of it was true). The problem was that his data was irrelevant; the conclusions he was trying to support weren't logically related to his evidence. That's why I think the Warren example is so good. It's demagoguery in its most dangerous form: when it comes packaged in facts and decorum.

I didn't write a whole book to help you identify the obvious demagoguery among us—the divisive, fact-free, in-group dogwhistling shouted by bullies. I wrote this book to show you how demagoguery can seem perfectly agreeable—and therefore, harder to spot and resist. And I wrote it to show you the way to defeat demagoguery in all its forms: not merely to be civil or to stick to facts but to vigilantly hold ourselves and others accountable to logic.

Warren is a hero of mine, in fact—for how elegantly he worked with the other Supreme Court justices in favor of justice when it came to *Brown v. Board of Education of Topeka*. His racist demagoguery, in regard to the mass imprisonment of Japanese Americans, shows that even good people can do very bad things, and that even very smart people can get suckered by demagoguery—including their own. Demagoguery isn't just a way to argue. It's a way we're tempted to think.

WORKS CITED AND RECOMMENDED

Allport, Gordon W. *The Nature of Prejudice*. Cambridge: Perseus, 1954.

Fromm, Erich. *Escape from Freedom*. New York: Hearst-Avon, 1941.

Gellately, Robert. *Backing Hitler: Consent and Coercion in Nazi Germany*. Oxford: Oxford University Press, 2001.

Haidt, Jonathan. *The Righteous Mind: Why Good People Are Divided by Politics and Religion*. New York: Pantheon, 2012.

Kahneman, Daniel. *Thinking, Fast and Slow*. New York: Farrar, Straus and Giroux, 2011.

Kashima, Tetsuden. *Judgment Without Trial: Japanese American Imprisonment During World War II*. Seattle: University of Washington Press, 2003.

Kershaw, Ian. *Hitler, the Germans, and the Final Solution*. New Haven: Yale University Press, 2008.

Lakoff, George. *Moral Politics: How Liberals and Conservatives Think*, 2nd ed. Chicago: University of Chicago Press, 1996.

Mann, Michael. *The Dark Side of Democracy: Explaining Ethnic Cleansing*. Cambridge: Cambridge University Press, 2005.

Martineau, Harriet. *Society in America*. London: Saunders and Otley, 1837.

Robinson, Greg. *A Tragedy of Democracy: Japanese Confinement in North America*. New York: Columbia University Press, 2009.

—. *By Order of the President: FDR and the Internment of Japanese Americans*. Cambridge: Harvard University Press, 2001.

Simms, William Gilmore. *Slavery in America: Being a Brief Review of Miss Martineau on That Subject*. Richmond: T. W. White, 1838.

Stratigakos, Despina. *Hitler at Home*. New Haven: Yale University Press, 2015.

Tetlock, Philip E. and Dan Gardner. *Superforecasting: The Art and Science of Prediction*. New York: Broadway Books, 2016.

Thucydides, trans. Steven Lattimore. *The Peloponnesian War*. Indianapolis: Hackett, 1998.

United States Commission on Wartime Relocation and Internment of Civilians. *Personal Justice Denied: Report of the Commission on Wartime Relocation and Internment of Civilians*. Washington, DC: Civil Liberties Public Education Fund; Seattle: University of Washington Press, 1997.

United States Congress, House, Select Committee Investigating National Defense Migration. *National Defense Migration Hearings*. 77th Cong., 2nd sess. Washington, DC: Government Printing Office, 1942.

Warren, Earl. *The Memoirs of Chief Justice Earl Warren*. Garden City: Doubleday, 1977.

Willner, Ann Ruth. *The Spellbinders: Charismatic Political Leadership*. New Haven and London: Yale University Press, 1984.

ACKNOWLEDGMENTS

It's impossible to acknowledge all the people who have significantly contributed to this book, especially family members, colleagues, and friends who argued with me about this issue for years. I'm particularly grateful to journals and conference organizers who published or promoted various versions of my thinking on this: *Rhetoric Society Quarterly* ("Dissent as 'Aid and Comfort to the Enemy': The Rhetorical Power of Naïve Realism and Ingroup Identity," 39, no. 2 [Spring 2009], 170–88) and *Rhetoric and Public Affairs* ("Democracy, Demagoguery, and Critical Rhetoric," 8 [2005]: 459–76). Tolerant audiences at various talks have encouraged, criticized, and usefully challenged this work, and I'm thankful that Carnegie Mellon University, University of Denver, University of Illinois, San Diego State University, Texas A&M, University of Tennessee, Michigan State University, and Furman University invited me to present parts of it, and National Communication Association, Rhetoric Society of America, and College Composition and Communication conferences have been invaluable sites for discussion and criticism.

ABOUT THE AUTHOR

PATRICIA ROBERTS-MILLER, PhD, is professor
of rhetoric and writing and director of the
University Writing Center at University of
Texas at Austin. She has been teaching the
subject of demagoguery since 2002 and is
also the author of *Voices in the Wilderness,*
*Deliberate Conflict, Fanatical Scheme*s and
Rhetoric and Demagoguery.